Healing Scriptures

Kenneth E. Hagin

Unless otherwise indicated, all Scripture quotations in this volume are from the *King James Version* of the Bible.

Second Printing 1993

ISBN 0-89276-521-6

In the U.S. write:
Kenneth Hagin Ministries
P.O. Box 50126
Tulsa, OK 74150-0126

In Canada write:
Kenneth Hagin Ministries
P.O. Box 335
Etobicoke (Toronto), Ontario
Canada, M9A 4X3

Following God's Plan For Your Life
The Triumphant Church
Healing Scriptures
Mountain Moving Faith
The Price Is Not Greater Than God's Grace (Mrs. Oretha Hagin)

MINIBOOKS (A partial listing)

* *The New Birth*
* *Why Tongues?*
* *In Him*
* *God's Medicine*
* *You Can Have What You Say*
  How To Write Your Own Ticket With God
* *Don't Blame God*
* *Words*
  Plead Your Case
* *How To Keep Your Healing*
  The Bible Way To Receive the Holy Spirit
  I Went to Hell
  How To Walk in Love
  The Precious Blood of Jesus
* *Love Never Fails*
  Your Faith in God Will Work

BOOKS BY KENNETH HAGIN JR.

* *Man's Impossibility — God's Possibility*
  Because of Jesus
  How To Make the Dream God Gave You Come True
  The Life of Obedience
  God's Irresistible Word
  Healing: Forever Settled
  Don't Quit! Your Faith Will See You Through
  The Untapped Power in Praise
  Listen to Your Heart
  What Comes After Faith?
  Speak to Your Mountain!
  Come Out of the Valley!

MINIBOOKS (A partial listing)

* *Faith Worketh by Love*
  Blueprint for Building Strong Faith
* *Seven Hindrances to Healing*
* *The Past Tense of God's Word*
  Faith Takes Back What the Devil's Stolen
  "The Prison Door Is Open — What Are You Still Doing Inside?"
  How To Be a Success in Life
  Get Acquainted With God
  Showdown With the Devil
  Unforgiveness
  Ministering to the Brokenhearted

*These titles are also available in Spanish. Information about other foreign translations of several of the above titles (i.e., Finnish, French, German, Indonesian, Polish, Russian, etc.) may be obtained by writing to: Kenneth Hagin Ministries, P.O. Box 50126, Tulsa, Oklahoma 74150-0126.

Contents

Preface

How often have you heard someone ask, "Why don't I get healed?"

This is a question that I often sense from those to whom I am ministering healing. The book you are about to read is my answer to that question.

Sickness is not a blessing, and it is not God's will! The Scriptures declare that sickness is a curse of the Law (Deut. 28:15, 61).

But I *know* that healing belongs to the New Testament Church, the Body of the Lord Jesus Christ, because the Scriptures also say that Christ has *redeemed* us from the curse of the Law, which includes *every* sickness and disease (Gal. 3:13). Therefore, I *know* that God wants His people well!

These *Healing Scriptures* were compiled because I believe that for Christians to receive the healing that God has provided for them through Jesus, their minds must be renewed to what the Word says about healing.

As you take "God's medicine" by meditating on His *Healing Scriptures*, I pray that your spirit will rise up strong within you and appropriate God's healing power for your body!

Chapter 1
God's Word Is God's Medicine

My son, attend to my words; incline thine ear unto my sayings.

Let them not depart from thine eyes; keep them in the midst of thine heart.

For they are life unto those that find them, and health to all their flesh.

— Proverbs 4:20-22

In the margin of my *King James* translation, Proverbs 4:22 reads, "My words are *medicine* to all their flesh." God's Word is medicine to all your flesh, but you need to learn how to *take* God's medicine in order to get it to work for you.

We know that faith comes by hearing, and hearing by the Word of God, because the Bible says so (Rom. 10:17). But to tell you the real truth about the matter, God's Word, His medicine, won't do you a bit of good in the world if you heard it over and over again for hours yet still continued to think wrong and talk wrong.

If you continue to think wrong and talk wrong, God's Word won't work for you. No, you've got to *hear* God's Word, because that's how faith comes, but then you've got to *act* on your faith.

1

So when you're confessing God's Word, if you would think like this: "I'm taking my medicine — God's Word. God's medicine always works. It never fails." Say that to yourself and think on *that*, and you'll get God's Word working in you.

Proverbs 4:20 says, *"My son, attend to my words; incline thine ear unto my sayings."* This is God speaking to you. He goes on to say, *"Let them* [God's words] *not depart from thine eyes; keep them in the midst of thine heart"* (v. 21). Why? So you can use God's words to condemn yourself? No! *"FOR THEY ARE LIFE unto those that find them, and HEALTH to all their flesh* (v. 22).

God's Word is medicine to *all* our flesh. That means there's not anything it won't cure. Therefore, I just want to give you God's medicine.

Read these scriptures out loud to yourself and meditate on them continually. You take God's medicine by doing what Proverbs 4:20 and 21 says to do: (1) *Attend* to God's Word; (2) *incline your ear* unto it; (3) *let it not depart* from your eyes; (4) *keep it* in the midst of your heart.

MATTHEW 6:9,10
9 ... Our Father which art in heaven, Hallowed be thy name.
10 Thy kingdom come. Thy will be done in earth, as it is in heaven.

Healing *is* God's will. The Bible says there is no sickness in Heaven. So we know from Matthew 6:10 that it's God's will that there be no sickness on earth.

3 JOHN 1:2
2   Beloved, I wish above all things that thou mayest prosper and be in health, even as thy soul prospereth.

1 JOHN 5:14,15
14 And this is the confidence that we have in him, that, if we ask any thing according to his will, he heareth us:
15 And if we know that he hear us, whatsoever we ask, we know that we have the petitions that we desired of him.

HEBREWS 12:12,13
12 Wherefore lift up the hands which hang down, and the feeble knees;
13 And make straight paths for your feet, lest that which is lame be turned out of the way; but let it rather be healed.

PHILIPPIANS 2:13
13 For it is God which worketh in you both to will and to do of his good pleasure.

ROMANS 8:32
32 He that spared not his own Son, but delivered him up for us all, how shall he not with him also freely give us all things?

JAMES 1:17
17 Every good gift and every perfect gift is from above, and cometh down from the Father of lights, with whom is no variableness, neither shadow of turning.

ROMANS 8:31
31 ... If God be for us, who can be against us?

MALACHI 3:6
6   For I am the Lord, I change not. ...

ISAIAH 41:10
10 Fear thou not; for I am with thee: be not dismayed; for I am thy God: I will strengthen thee; yea, I will help thee; yea, I will uphold thee with the right hand of my righteousness.

DEUTERONOMY 7:15
15 And the Lord will take away from thee all sickness, and will put none [permit none] of the evil diseases of Egypt, which thou knowest, upon thee.

EXODUS 15:26
26 ... If thou wilt diligently hearken to the voice of the Lord thy God, and wilt do that which is right in his sight, and wilt give ear to his commandments, and keep all his statutes, I will put none [permit none] of these diseases upon thee, which I have permitted upon the Egyptians: for I am the Lord that healeth thee.

JEREMIAH 30:17
17 For I will restore health unto thee, and I will heal thee of thy wounds, saith the Lord. . . .

JEREMIAH 33:6
6 Behold, I will bring it health and cure, and I will cure them, and will reveal unto them the abundance of peace and truth.

DEUTERONOMY 30:19,20
19 I call heaven and earth to record this day against you, that I have set before you life and death, blessing and cursing: therefore choose life, that both thou and thy seed may live:
20 That thou mayest love the Lord thy God, and that thou mayest obey his voice, and that thou mayest cleave unto him: for he is thy life, and the length of thy days: that thou mayest dwell in the land which the Lord sware unto thy fathers. . . .

LEVITICUS 26:3,9
3 If ye walk in my statutes, and keep my commandments, and do them. . . .
9 . . . I will have respect unto you, and make you fruitful, and multiply you, and establish my covenant with you.

ISAIAH 58:8
8 Then shall thy light break forth as the morning, and thine health shall spring forth speedily: and thy righteousness shall go before thee; the glory of the Lord shall be thy rereward.

GENESIS 20:17
17 So Abraham prayed unto God: and God healed Abimelech, and his wife, and his maidservants; and they bare children.

2 CHRONICLES 30:20
20 And the Lord hearkened to Hezekiah, and healed the people.

2 KINGS 20:5
5   Turn again, and tell Hezekiah the captain of my people, Thus saith the Lord, the God of David thy father, I have heard thy prayer, I have seen thy tears: behold, I will heal thee....

NUMBERS 23:19
19 God is not a man, that he should lie; neither the son of man, that he should repent: hath he said, and shall he not do it? or hath he spoken, and shall he not make it good?

2 CHRONICLES 6:14
14 ... O Lord God of Israel, there is no God like thee in the heaven, nor in the earth; which keepest covenant, and shewest mercy unto thy servants, that walk before thee with all their hearts.

2 CHRONICLES 16:9
9   For the eyes of the Lord run to and fro throughout the whole earth, to shew himself strong in the behalf of them whose heart is perfect toward him....

PSALM 145:8,9
8   The Lord is gracious, and full of compassion;
slow to anger, and of great mercy.
9   The Lord is good to all: and his tender mercies
are over all his works.

JOB 37:23
23 Touching the Almighty . . . he is excellent in
power, and in judgment, and in plenty of justice:
he will not afflict.

PSALM 67:2
2   That thy way may be known upon earth, thy
saving health among all nations.

PSALM 105:37
37 He brought them forth also with silver and
gold: and there was not one feeble person among
their tribes.

PSALM 103:3
3   Who forgiveth all thine iniquities; who healeth
all thy diseases.

PSALM 147:3
3   He healeth the broken in heart, and bindeth
up their wounds.

PSALM 23:1
1   The Lord is my shepherd; I shall not want.

PSALM 30:2
2   O Lord my God, I cried unto thee, and thou
hast healed me.

PSALM 34:19
19 Many are the afflictions of the righteous: but
the Lord delivereth him out of them all.

PSALM 41:3
3   The Lord will strengthen him upon the bed of
languishing. . . .

PSALM 42:11
11 . . . hope thou in God: for I shall yet praise him,
who is the health of my countenance, and my
God.

MATTHEW 7:11
11 If ye then, being evil, know how to give good
gifts unto your children, how much more shall
your Father which is in heaven give good things
to them that ask him?

Healing Is in the Plan of Redemption

ISAIAH 53:4,5
4   **Surely he** [Jesus] **hath borne our griefs, and
carried our sorrows** [literal Hebrew: Surely He has
lifted, carried, or borne our sicknesses or diseases and
our pain]**: yet we did esteem him stricken, smitten
of God, and afflicted.**

5   But he was wounded for our transgressions, he was bruised for our iniquities: the chastisement of our peace was upon him; and with his stripes we are healed.

MATTHEW 8:17
17 That it might be fulfilled which was spoken by Isaiah the prophet, saying, Himself took our infirmities, and bare our sicknesses.

1 PETER 2:24
24 Who his own self bare our sins in his own body on the tree, that we, being dead to sins, should live unto righteousness: by whose stripes ye were healed.

GALATIANS 3:13,14,29
13 Christ hath redeemed us from the curse of the law, being made a curse for us: for it is written, Cursed is every one that hangeth on a tree:
14 That the blessing of Abraham might come on the Gentiles through Jesus Christ; that we might receive the promise of the Spirit through faith. . . .
29 And if ye be Christ's, then are ye Abraham's seed, and heirs according to the promise.

COLOSSIANS 1:12-14
12 Giving thanks unto the Father, which hath made us meet [or able] to be partakers of the inheritance of the saints in light:

13 Who hath delivered us from the power of darkness, and hath translated us into the kingdom of his dear Son:
14 In whom we have redemption through his blood, even the forgiveness of sins.

COLOSSIANS 2:10,15
10 And ye are complete in him, which is the head of all principality and power....
15 And having spoiled principalities and powers, he made a shew of them openly, triumphing over them in it.

HEBREWS 9:12
12 Neither by the blood of goats and calves, but by his own blood he entered in once into the holy place, having obtained eternal redemption for us.

Healing and Long Life — God's Will for You!

EPHESIANS 5:30
30 For we are members of his body, of his flesh, and of his bones.

1 THESSALONIANS 5:23
23 . . . And the very God of peace sanctify you wholly; and I pray God your whole spirit and soul and body be preserved blameless unto the coming of our Lord Jesus Christ.

HOSEA 13:14
14 I will ransom them from the power of the grave; I will redeem them from death: O death, I will be thy plagues; O grave, I will be thy destruction. . . .

EXODUS 20:12
12 Honour thy father and thy mother: that thy days may be long upon the land which the Lord thy God giveth thee.

DEUTERONOMY 5:33
33 Ye shall walk in all the ways which the Lord your God hath commanded you, that ye may live, and that it may be well with you, and that ye may prolong your days in the land which ye shall possess.

DEUTERONOMY 11:21
21 That your days may be multiplied, and the days of your children, in the land which the Lord sware unto your fathers to give them, as the days of heaven upon the earth.

1 CHRONICLES 29:28
28 And he [David] died in a good old age, full of days, riches, and honour. . . .

JOB 5:26
26 Thou shalt come to thy grave in a full age, like as a shock of corn cometh in in his season.

PSALM 90:10
10 The days of our years are threescore years and ten; and if by reason of strength they be fourscore years. . . .

PSALM 91:10-16
10 There shall no evil befall thee, neither shall any plague come nigh thy dwelling.
11 For he shall give his angels charge over thee, to keep thee in all thy ways.
12 They shall bear thee up in their hands, lest thou dash thy foot against a stone.
13 Thou shalt tread upon the lion and adder: the young lion and the dragon shalt thou trample under feet.
14 Because he hath set his love upon me, therefore will I deliver him: I will set him on high, because he hath known my name.
15 He shall call upon me, and I will answer him: I will be with him in trouble; I will deliver him, and honour him.
16 With long life will I satisfy him, and shew him my salvation.

PROVERBS 3:1,2
1 My son, forget not my law; but let thine heart keep my commandments:
2 For length of days, and long life, and peace, shall they add to thee.

PROVERBS 9:11
11 For by me thy days shall be multiplied, and the years of thy life shall be increased.

ECCLESIASTES 7:17
17 . . . why shouldest thou die before thy time?

ISAIAH 40:31
31 But they that wait upon the Lord shall renew their strength; they shall mount up with wings as eagles; they shall run, and not be weary; and they shall walk, and not faint.

ISAIAH 65:22
22 They shall not build, and another inhabit; they shall not plant, and another eat: for as the days of a tree are the days of my people, and mine elect shall long enjoy the work of their hands.

EPHESIANS 6:1-3
1 Children, obey your parents in the Lord: for this is right.
2 Honour thy father and mother; which is the first commandment with promise;
3 That it may be well with thee, and thou mayest live long on the earth.

So you see, God has promised us long life, and He wants us to have long life.

Chapter 2
Jesus — The Will of God In Action

Now let's look at some scriptures concerning the earth walk of Jesus and His healing ministry.

MATTHEW 4:23,24
23 And Jesus went about all Galilee, teaching in their synagogues, and preaching the gospel of the kingdom, and healing all manner of sickness and all manner of disease among the people.
24 And his fame went throughout all Syria: and they brought unto him all sick people that were taken with divers diseases and torments, and those which were possessed with devils, and those which were lunatick, and those that had the palsy; and he healed them.

MATTHEW 8:2,3
2   And, behold, there came a leper and worshipped him, saying, Lord, if thou wilt, thou canst make me clean.
3   And Jesus put forth his hand, and touched him, saying, I will; be thou clean. And immediately his leprosy was cleansed.

MATTHEW 8:5-10,13
5   And when Jesus was entered into Capernaum,

there came unto him a centurion, beseeching him,
6   And saying, Lord, my servant lieth at home sick of the palsy, grievously tormented.
7   And Jesus saith unto him, I will come and heal him.
8   The centurion answered and said, Lord, I am not worthy that thou shouldest come under my roof: but speak the word only, and my servant shall be healed.
9   For I am a man under authority, having soldiers under me: and I say to this man, Go, and he goeth; and to another, Come, and he cometh; and to my servant, Do this, and he doeth it.
10 When Jesus heard it, he marvelled, and said to them that followed, Verily I say unto you, I have not found so great faith, no, not in Israel. . . .
13 And Jesus said unto the centurion, Go thy way; and as thou hast believed, so be it done unto thee. And his servant was healed in the selfsame hour.

MATTHEW 8:14-17
14 And when Jesus was come into Peter's house, he saw his wife's mother laid, and sick of a fever.
15 And he touched her hand, and the fever left her: and she arose, and ministered unto them
16 When the even was come, they brought unto him many that were possessed with devils: and he cast out the spirits with his word, and healed all that were sick:
17 That it might be fulfilled which was spoken by Esaias the prophet, saying, Himself took our infirmities, and bare our sicknesses.

MATTHEW 9:20-22

20 And, behold, a woman, which was diseased with an issue of blood twelve years, came behind him, and touched the hem of his garment:

21 For she said within herself, If I may but touch his garment, I shall be whole.

22 But Jesus turned him about, and when he saw her, he said, Daughter, be of good comfort; thy faith hath made thee whole. And the woman was made whole from that hour.

MATTHEW 9:27-36

27 And when Jesus departed thence, two blind men followed him, crying, and saying, Thou son of David, have mercy on us.

28 And when he was come into the house, the blind men came to him: and Jesus saith unto them, Believe ye that I am able to do this? They said unto him, Yea, Lord.

29 Then touched he their eyes, saying, According to your faith be it unto you.

30 And their eyes were opened; and Jesus straitly charged them, saying, See that no man know it.

31 But they, when they were departed, spread abroad his fame in all that country.

32 As they went out, behold, they brought to him a dumb man possessed with a devil.

33 And when the devil was cast out, the dumb spake: and the multitudes marvelled, saying, It was never so seen in Israel.

34 But the Pharisees said, He casteth out devils

through the prince of the devils.

35 And Jesus went about all the cities and villages, teaching in their synagogues, and preaching the gospel of the kingdom, and healing every sickness and every disease among the people.

36 But when he saw the multitudes, he was moved with compassion on them, because they fainted, and were scattered abroad, as sheep having no shepherd.

MATTHEW 11:28-30

28 Come unto me, all ye that labour and are heavy laden, and I will give you rest.

29 Take my yoke upon you, and learn of me; for I am meek and lowly in heart: and ye shall find rest unto your souls.

30 For my yoke is easy, and my burden is light.

MATTHEW 12:15

15 But when Jesus knew it, he withdrew himself from thence: and great multitudes followed him, and he healed them all.

MATTHEW 14:13,14

13 When Jesus heard of it, he departed thence by ship into a desert place apart: and when the people had heard thereof, they followed him on foot out of the cities.

14 And Jesus went forth, and saw a great multitude, and was moved with compassion toward them, and he healed their sick.

MATTHEW 14:34-36

34 And when they were gone over, they came into the land of Gennesaret.

35 And when the men of that place had knowledge of him, they sent out into all that country round about, and brought unto him all that were diseased;

36 And besought him that they might only touch the hem of his garment: and as many as touched were made perfectly whole.

MATTHEW 15:29-31

29 And Jesus departed from thence, and came nigh unto the sea of Galilee; and went up into a mountain, and sat down there.

30 And great multitudes came unto him, having with them those that were lame, blind, dumb, maimed, and many others, and cast them down at Jesus' feet; and he healed them:

31 Insomuch that the multitude wondered, when they saw the dumb to speak, the maimed to be whole, the lame to walk, and the blind to see: and they glorified the God of Israel.

MARK 5:1-43

1 And they came over unto the other side of the sea, into the country of the Gadarenes.

2 And when he was come out of the ship, immediately there met him out of the tombs a man with an unclean spirit,

3   Who had his dwelling among the tombs; and
no man could bind him, no, not with chains:
4   Because that he had been often bound with
fetters and chains, and the chains had been
plucked asunder by him, and the fetters broken
in pieces: neither could any man tame him.
5   And always, night and day, he was in the
mountains, and in the tombs, crying, and cutting
himself with stones.
6   But when he saw Jesus afar off, he ran and
worshipped him,
7   And cried with a loud voice, and said, What
have I to do with thee, Jesus, thou Son of the
most high God? I adjure thee by God, that thou
torment me not.
8   For he said unto him, Come out of the man,
thou unclean spirit.
9   And he asked him, What is thy name? And he
answered, saying, My name is Legion: for we are
many.
10 And he besought him much that he would not
send them away out of the country.
11 Now there was there nigh unto the mountains
a great herd of swine feeding.
12 And all the devils besought him, saying, Send
us into the swine, that we may enter into them.
13 And forthwith Jesus gave them leave. And the
unclean spirits went out, and entered into the
swine: and the herd ran violently down a steep
place into the sea, (they were about two thousand;) and were choked in the sea.
14 And they that fed the swine fled, and told it in

the city, and in the country. And they went out to see what it was that was done.

15 And they come to Jesus, and see him that was possessed with the devil, and had the legion, sitting, and clothed, and in his right mind: and they were afraid.

16 And they that saw it told them how it befell to him that was possessed with the devil, and also concerning the swine.

17 And they began to pray him to depart out of their coasts.

18 And when he was come into the ship, he that had been possessed with the devil prayed him that he might be with him.

19 Howbeit Jesus suffered him not, but saith unto him, Go home to thy friends, and tell them how great things the Lord hath done for thee, and hath had compassion on thee.

20 And he departed, and began to publish in Decapolis how great things Jesus had done for him: and all men did marvel.

21 And when Jesus was passed over again by ship unto the other side, much people gathered unto him: and he was nigh unto the sea.

22 And, behold, there cometh one of the rulers of the synagogue, Jairus by name; and when he saw him, he fell at his feet,

23 And besought him greatly, saying, My little daughter lieth at the point of death: I pray thee, come and lay thy hands on her, that she may be healed; and she shall live.

24 And Jesus went with him; and much people

followed him, and thronged him.

25 And a certain woman, which had an issue of blood twelve years,

26 And had suffered many things of many physicians, and had spent all that she had, and was nothing bettered, but rather grew worse,

27 When she had heard of Jesus, came in the press behind, and touched his garment.

28 For she said, If I may touch but his clothes, I shall be whole.

29 And straightway the fountain of her blood was dried up; and she felt in her body that she was healed of that plague.

30 And Jesus, immediately knowing in himself that virtue had gone out of him, turned him about in the press, and said, Who touched my clothes?

31 And his disciples said unto him, Thou seest the multitude thronging thee, and sayest thou, Who touched me?

32 And he looked round about to see her that had done this thing.

33 But the woman fearing and trembling, knowing what was done in her, came and fell down before him, and told him all the truth.

34 And he said unto her, Daughter, thy faith hath made thee whole; go in peace, and be whole of thy plague.

35 While he yet spake, there came from the ruler of the synagogue's house certain which said, Thy daughter is dead: why troublest thou the Master any further?

36 As soon as Jesus heard the word that was spoken, he saith unto the ruler of the synagogue, Be not afraid, only believe.

37 And he suffered no man to follow him, save Peter, and James, and John the brother of James.

38 And he cometh to the house of the ruler of the synagogue, and seeth the tumult, and them that wept and wailed greatly.

39 And when he was come in, he saith unto them, Why make ye this ado, and weep? the damsel is not dead, but sleepeth.

40 And they laughed him to scorn. But when he had put them all out, he taketh the father and the mother of the damsel, and them that were with him, and entereth in where the damsel was lying.

41 And he took the damsel by the hand, and said unto her, Talitha cumi; which is, being interpreted, Damsel, I say unto thee, arise.

42 And straightway the damsel arose, and walked; for she was of the age of twelve years. And they were astonished with a great astonishment.

43 And he charged them straitly that no man should know it; and commanded that something should be given her to eat.

MARK 6:53-56

53 And when they had passed over, they came into the land of Gennesaret, and drew to the shore.

54 And when they were come out of the ship, straightway they knew him,

55 And ran through that whole region round about, and began to carry about in beds those that were sick, where they heard he was.

56 And whithersoever he entered, into villages, or cities, or country, they laid the sick in the streets, and besought him that they might touch if it were but the border of his garment: and as many as touched him were made whole.

MARK 7:25-37

25 For a certain woman, whose young daughter had an unclean spirit, heard of him, and came and fell at his feet:

26 The woman was a Greek, a Syrophenician by nation; and she besought him that he would cast forth the devil out of her daughter.

27 But Jesus said unto her, Let the children first be filled: for it is not meet to take the children's bread, and to cast it unto the dogs.

28 And she answered and said unto him, Yes, Lord: yet the dogs under the table eat of the children's crumbs.

29 And he said unto her, For this saying go thy way; the devil is gone out of thy daughter.

30 And when she was come to her house, she found the devil gone out, and her daughter laid upon the bed.

31 And again, departing from the coasts of Tyre and Sidon, he came unto the sea of Galilee,

through the midst of the coasts of Decapolis.

32 And they bring unto him one that was deaf, and had an impediment in his speech; and they beseech him to put his hand upon him.

33 And he took him aside from the multitude, and put his fingers into his ears, and he spit, and touched his tongue;

34 And looking up to heaven, he sighed, and saith unto him, Ephphatha, that is, Be opened.

35 And straightway his ears were opened, and the string of his tongue was loosed, and he spake plain.

36 And he charged them that they should tell no man: but the more he charged them, so much the more a great deal they published it;

37 And were beyond measure astonished, saying, He hath done all things well: he maketh both the deaf to hear, and the dumb to speak.

MARK 9:17-29

17 And one of the multitude answered and said, Master, I have brought unto thee my son, which hath a dumb spirit;

18 And wheresoever he taketh him, he teareth him: and he foameth, and gnasheth with his teeth, and pineth away: and I spake to thy disciples that they should cast him out; and they could not.

19 He answereth him, and saith, O faithless generation, how long shall I be with you? how long shall I suffer you? bring him unto me.

20 And they brought him unto him: and when he

saw him, straightway the spirit tare him; and he
fell on the ground, and wallowed foaming.

21 And he asked his father, How long is it ago
since this came unto him? And he said, Of a child.

22 And ofttimes it hath cast him into the fire, and
into the waters, to destroy him: but if thou canst
do any thing, have compassion on us, and help us.

23 Jesus said unto him, If thou canst believe, all
things are possible to him that believeth.

24 And straightway the father of the child cried
out, and said with tears, Lord, I believe; help thou
mine unbelief.

25 When Jesus saw that the people came running
together, he rebuked the foul spirit, saying unto
him, Thou dumb and deaf spirit, I charge thee,
come out of him, and enter no more into him.

26 And the spirit cried, and rent him sore, and
came out of him: and he was as one dead; insomuch that many said, He is dead.

27 But Jesus took him by the hand, and lifted
him up; and he arose.

28 And when he was come into the house, his disciples asked him privately, Why could not we cast
him out?

29 And he said unto them, This kind can come
forth by nothing, but by prayer and fasting.

LUKE 4:16-21
16 And he came to Nazareth, where he had been
brought up: and, as his custom was, he went into
the synagogue on the sabbath day, and stood up
for to read.

17 And there was delivered unto him the book of the prophet Esaias. And when he had opened the book, he found the place where it was written,
18 The Spirit of the Lord is upon me, because he hath anointed me to preach the gospel to the poor; he hath sent me to heal the brokenhearted, to preach deliverance to the captives, and recovering of sight to the blind, to set at liberty them that are bruised,
19 To preach the acceptable year of the Lord.
20 And he closed the book, and he gave it again to the minister, and sat down. And the eyes of all them that were in the synagogue were fastened on him.
21 And he began to say unto them, This day is this scripture fulfilled in your ears.

LUKE 4:33-36,40,41
33 And in the synagogue there was a man, which had a spirit of an unclean devil, and cried out with a loud voice,
34 Saying, Let us alone; what have we to do with thee, thou Jesus of Nazareth? art thou come to destroy us? I know thee who thou art; the Holy One of God.
35 And Jesus rebuked him, saying, Hold thy peace, and come out of him. And when the devil had thrown him in the midst, he came out of him, and hurt him not.
36 And they were all amazed, and spake among themselves, saying, What a word is this! for with

authority and power he commandeth the unclean
spirits, and they come out. . . .
40 Now when the sun was setting, all they that
had any sick with divers diseases brought them
unto him; and he laid his hands on every one of
them, and healed them.
41 And devils also came out of many, crying out,
and saying, Thou art Christ the Son of God. And
he rebuking them suffered them not to speak: for
they knew that he was Christ.

LUKE 6:6-10
6   And it came to pass also on another sabbath,
that he entered into the synagogue and taught:
and there was a man whose right hand was withered.
7   And the scribes and Pharisees watched him,
whether he would heal on the sabbath day; that
they might find an accusation against him.
8   But he knew their thoughts, and said to the
man which had the withered hand, Rise up, and
stand forth in the midst. And he arose and stood
forth.
9   Then said Jesus unto them, I will ask you one
thing; Is it lawful on the sabbath days to do good,
or to do evil? to save life, or to destroy it?
10 And looking round about upon them all, he
said unto the man, Stretch forth thy hand. And he
did so: and his hand was restored whole as the
other.

LUKE 6:17-19

17 And he came down with them, and stood in the plain, and the company of his disciples, and a great multitude of people out of all Judaea and Jerusalem, and from the sea coast of Tyre and Sidon, which came to hear him, and to be healed of their diseases;

18 And they that were vexed with unclean spirits: and they were healed.

19 And the whole multitude sought to touch him: for there went virtue out of him, and healed them all.

LUKE 13:11-17

11 And, behold, there was a woman which had a spirit of infirmity eighteen years, and was bowed together, and could in no wise lift up herself.

12 And when Jesus saw her, he called her to him, and said unto her, Woman, thou art loosed from thine infirmity.

13 And he laid his hands on her: and immediately she was made straight, and glorified God.

14 And the ruler of the synagogue answered with indignation, because that Jesus had healed on the sabbath day, and said unto the people, There are six days in which men ought to work: in them therefore come and be healed, and not on the sabbath day.

15 The Lord then answered him, and said, Thou hypocrite, doth not each one of you on the sabbath loose his ox or his ass from the stall, and

lead him away to watering?

16 And ought not this woman, being a daughter of Abraham, whom Satan hath bound, lo, these eighteen years, be loosed from this bond on the sabbath day?

17 And when he had said these things, all his adversaries were ashamed: and all the people rejoiced for all the glorious things that were done by him.

JOHN 5:2-14

2 Now there is at Jerusalem by the sheep market a pool, which is called in the Hebrew tongue Bethesda, having five porches.

3 In these lay a great multitude of impotent folk, of blind, halt, withered, waiting for the moving of the water.

4 For an angel went down at a certain season into the pool, and troubled the water: whosoever then first after the troubling of the water stepped in was made whole of whatsoever disease he had.

5 And a certain man was there, which had an infirmity thirty and eight years.

6 When Jesus saw him lie, and knew that he had been now a long time in that case, he saith unto him, Wilt thou be made whole?

7 The impotent man answered him, Sir, I have no man, when the water is troubled, to put me into the pool: but while I am coming, another steppeth down before me.

8 Jesus saith unto him, Rise, take up thy bed, and walk.

9   And immediately the man was made whole, and took up his bed, and walked: and on the same day was the sabbath.

10 The Jews therefore said unto him that was cured, It is the sabbath day: it is not lawful for thee to carry thy bed.

11 He answered them, He that made me whole, the same said unto me, Take up thy bed, and walk.

12 Then asked they him, What man is that which said unto thee, Take up thy bed, and walk?

13 And he that was healed wist not who it was: for Jesus had conveyed himself away, a multitude being in that place.

14 Afterward Jesus findeth him in the temple, and said unto him, Behold, thou art made whole: sin no more, lest a worse thing come unto thee.

JOHN 9:1-7

1   And as Jesus passed by, he saw a man which was blind from his birth.

2   And his disciples asked him, saying, Master, who did sin, this man, or his parents, that he was born blind?

3   Jesus answered, Neither hath this man sinned, nor his parents: but that the works of God should be made manifest in him.

4   I must work the works of him that sent me, while it is day: the night cometh, when no man can work.

5   As long as I am in the world, I am the light of the world.

6   When he had thus spoken, he spat on the ground, and made clay of the spittle, and he anointed the eyes of the blind man with the clay,
7   And said unto him, Go, wash in the pool of Siloam, (which is by interpretation, Sent.) He went his way therefore, and washed, and came seeing.

JOHN 10:10
10 The thief cometh not, but for to steal, and to kill, and to destroy: I am come that they might have life, and that they might have it more abundantly.

ACTS 10:38
38 How God anointed Jesus of Nazareth with the Holy Ghost and with power: who went about doing good, and healing all that were oppressed of the devil; for God was with him.

HEBREWS 13:8
8   Jesus Christ the same yesterday, and to day, and for ever.

1 JOHN 3:8
8   He that committeth sin is of the devil; for the devil sinneth from the beginning. For this purpose the Son of God was manifested, that he might destroy the works of the devil.

MATTHEW 10:1
1 And when he had called unto him his twelve disciples, he gave them power against unclean spirits, to cast them out, and to heal all manner of sickness and all manner of disease.

MARK 16:15-20
15 And he said unto them, Go ye into all the world, and preach the gospel to every creature.
16 He that believeth and is baptized shall be saved; but he that believeth not shall be damned.
17 And these signs shall follow them that believe; In my name shall they cast out devils; they shall speak with new tongues;
18 They shall take up serpents; and if they drink any deadly thing, it shall not hurt them; they shall lay hands on the sick, and they shall recover.
19 So then after the Lord had spoken unto them, he was received up into heaven, and sat on the right hand of God.
20 And they went forth, and preached every where, the Lord working with them, and confirming the word with signs following. . . .

Chapter 3
Healing Is One of the 'Greater Works'

JOHN 14:12-15
12 Verily, verily, I say unto you, He that believeth on me, the works that I do shall he do also; and greater works than these shall he do; because I go unto my Father.
13 And whatsoever ye shall ask in my name, that will I do, that the Father may be glorified in the Son.
14 If ye shall ask any thing in my name, I will do it.
15 If ye love me, keep my commandments.

ACTS 6:8
8 And Stephen, full of faith and power, did great wonders and miracles among the people.

ACTS 8:6,7
6 And the people with one accord gave heed unto those things which Philip spake, hearing and seeing the miracles which he did.
7 For unclean spirits, crying with loud voice, came out of many that were possessed with them: and many taken with palsies, and that were lame, were healed.

ACTS 9:33,34
33 And there he found a certain man named Aeneas, which had kept his bed eight years, and was sick of the palsy.
34 And Peter said unto him, Aeneas, Jesus Christ maketh thee whole: arise, and make thy bed. And he arose immediately.

ACTS 14:8-10
8 And there sat a certain man at Lystra, impotent in his feet, being a cripple from his mother's womb, who never had walked:
9 The same heard Paul speak: who stedfastly beholding him, and perceiving that he had faith to be healed,
10 Said with a loud voice, Stand upright on thy feet. And he leaped and walked.

ACTS 19:11,12
11 And God wrought special miracles by the hands of Paul:
12 So that from his body were brought unto the sick handkerchiefs or aprons, and the diseases departed from them, and the evil spirits went out of them.

JAMES 5:14-16
14 Is any sick among you? let him call for the elders of the church; and let them pray over him, anointing him with oil in the name of the Lord:
15 And the prayer of faith shall save the sick, and

the Lord shall raise him up; and if he have committed sins, they shall be forgiven him.

16 Confess your faults one to another, and pray one for another, that ye may be healed. The effectual fervent prayer of a righteous man availeth much.

Believe and Accept the Healing
That Belongs to You in Christ!

MALACHI 4:2
2 But unto you that fear my name shall the Sun of righteousness arise with healing in his wings; and ye shall go forth, and grow up as calves of the stall.

HEBREWS 1:1-4
1 God, who at sundry times and in divers manners spake in time past unto the fathers by the prophets,
2 Hath in these last days spoken unto us by his Son, whom he hath appointed heir of all things, by whom also he made the worlds;
3 Who being the brightness of his glory, and the express image of his person, and upholding all things by the word of his power, when he had by himself purged our sins, sat down on the right hand of the Majesty on high;
4 Being made so much better than the angels, as he hath by inheritance obtained a more excellent name than they.

PHILIPPIANS 2:8-11

8   And being found in fashion as a man, he hum-
bled himself, and became obedient unto death,
even the death of the cross.

9   Wherefore God also hath highly exalted him,
and given him a name which is above every name:

10 That at the name of Jesus every knee should
bow, of things in heaven, and things in earth, and
things under the earth;

11 And that every tongue should confess that
Jesus Christ is Lord, to the glory of God the
Father.

EPHESIANS 1:16-23

16 Cease not to give thanks for you, making men-
tion of you in my prayers;

17 That the God of our Lord Jesus Christ, the
Father of glory, may give unto you the spirit of
wisdom and revelation in the knowledge of him:

18 The eyes of your understanding being enlight-
ened; that ye may know what is the hope of his
calling, and what the riches of the glory of his
inheritance in the saints,

19 And what is the exceeding greatness of his
power to usward who believe, according to the
working of his mighty power,

20 Which he wrought in Christ, when he raised
him from the dead, and set him at his own right
hand in the heavenly places,

21 Far above all principality, and power, and
might, and dominion, and every name that is

named, not only in this world, but also in that
which is to come:
22 And hath put all things under his feet, and gave
him to be the head over all things to the church,
23 Which is his body, the fulness of him that fil-
leth all in all.

There's Healing in Jesus' Name

JOHN 16:23,24
23 And in that day ye shall ask me nothing. Verily, verily, I say unto you, Whatsoever ye shall ask
the Father in my name, he will give it you.
24 Hitherto have ye asked nothing in my name:
ask, and ye shall receive, that your joy may be full.

MARK 16:15-18
15 And he said unto them, Go ye into all the
world, and preach the gospel to every creature.
16 He that believeth and is baptized shall be
saved; but he that believeth not shall be damned.
17 And these signs shall follow them that believe;
In my name shall they cast out devils; they shall
speak with new tongues;
18 They shall take up serpents; and if they drink
any deadly thing, it shall not hurt them; they shall
lay hands on the sick, and they shall recover.

Notice Jesus said, ". . . *in MY NAME . . . they shall
lay hands on the sick, and they shall recover"* (Mark
16:17,18). There is healing in the Name of Jesus. Why?

Because healing belongs to us. Jesus already provided it for us in our redemption.

JOHN 14:13,14

13 And whatsoever ye shall ask in my name, that will I do, that the Father may be glorified in the Son.

14 If ye shall ask any thing in my name, I will do it.

ACTS 3:1-16

1   Now Peter and John went up together into the temple at the hour of prayer, being the ninth hour.

2   And a certain man lame from his mother's womb was carried, whom they laid daily at the gate of the temple which is called Beautiful, to ask alms of them that entered into the temple;

3   Who seeing Peter and John about to go into the temple asked an alms.

4   And Peter, fastening his eyes upon him with John, said, Look on us.

5   And he gave heed unto them, expecting to receive something of them.

6   Then Peter said, Silver and gold have I none; but such as I have give I thee: In the name of Jesus Christ of Nazareth rise up and walk.

7   And he took him by the right hand, and lifted him up: and immediately his feet and ankle bones received strength.

8   And he leaping up stood, and walked, and

entered with them into the temple, walking, and leaping, and praising God.

9 And all the people saw him walking and praising God:

10 And they knew that it was he which sat for alms at the Beautiful gate of the temple: and they were filled with wonder and amazement at that which had happened unto him.

11 And as the lame man which was healed held Peter and John, all the people ran together unto them in the porch that is called Solomon's, greatly wondering.

12 And when Peter saw it, he answered unto the people, Ye men of Israel, why marvel ye at this? or why look ye so earnestly on us, as though by our own power or holiness we had made this man to walk?

13 The God of Abraham, and of Isaac, and of Jacob, the God of our fathers, hath glorified his Son Jesus; whom ye delivered up, and denied him in the presence of Pilate, when he was determined to let him go.

14 But ye denied the Holy One and the Just, and desired a murderer to be granted unto you;

15 And killed the Prince of life, whom God hath raised from the dead; whereof we are witnesses.

16 And his name through faith in his name [now notice that, And His Name, through *faith* in His Name] hath made this man strong, whom ye see and know: yea, the faith which is by him hath given him this perfect soundness in the presence of you all.

ACTS 4:1-18,23,24,29,30
1   And as they spake unto the people, the priests, and the captain of the temple, and the Sadducees, came upon them,
2   Being grieved that they taught the people, and preached through Jesus the resurrection from the dead.
3   And they laid hands on them, and put them in hold unto the next day: for it was now eventide.
4   Howbeit many of them which heard the word believed; and the number of the men was about five thousand.
5   And it came to pass on the morrow, that their rulers, and elders, and scribes,
6   And Annas the high priest, and Caiaphas, and John, and Alexander, and as many as were of the kindred of the high priest, were gathered together at Jerusalem.
7   And when they had set them in the midst, they asked, By what power, or by what name, have ye done this?
8   Then Peter, filled with the Holy Ghost, said unto them, Ye rulers of the people, and elders of Israel,
9   If we this day be examined of the good deed done to the impotent man, by what means he is made whole;
10 Be it known unto you all, and to all the people of Israel, that by the name of Jesus Christ of Nazareth, whom ye crucified, whom God raised from the dead, even by him doth this man stand here before you whole.

11 This is the stone which was set at nought of you builders, which is become the head of the corner.

12 Neither is there salvation in any other: for there is none other name under heaven given among men, whereby we must be saved.

13 Now when they saw the boldness of Peter and John, and perceived that they were unlearned and ignorant men, they marvelled; and they took knowledge of them, that they had been with Jesus.

14 And beholding the man which was healed standing with them, they could say nothing against it.

15 But when they had commanded them to go aside out of the council, they conferred among themselves,

16 Saying, What shall we do to these men? for that indeed a notable miracle hath been done by them is manifest to all them that dwell in Jerusalem; and we cannot deny it.

17 But that it spread no further among the people, let us straitly threaten them, that they speak henceforth to no man in this name.

18 And they called them, and commanded them not to speak at all nor teach in the name of Jesus. . . .

23 And being let go, they went to their own company, and reported all that the chief priests and elders had said unto them.

24 And when they heard that, they lifted up their voice to God with one accord, and said . . .

29 And now, Lord, behold their threatenings: and grant unto thy servants, THAT WITH ALL BOLDNESS THEY MAY SPEAK THY WORD,
30 By stretching forth thine hand to heal; AND THAT SIGNS AND WONDERS MAY BE DONE BY THE NAME OF THY HOLY CHILD JESUS.

Receive Healing by Faith

MATTHEW 18:19
19 Again I say unto you, That if two of you shall agree on earth as touching any thing that they shall ask, it shall be done for them of my Father which is in heaven.

MARK 11:22-26
22 And Jesus answering saith unto them, Have faith in God.
23 For verily I say unto you, That whosoever shall say unto this mountain, Be thou removed, and be thou cast into the sea; and shall not doubt in his heart, but shall believe that those things which he saith shall come to pass; he shall have whatsoever he saith.
24 Therefore I say unto you, What things soever ye desire, when ye pray, believe that ye receive them, and ye shall have them.
25 And when ye stand praying, forgive, if ye have ought against any: that your Father also which is in heaven may forgive you your trespasses.
26 But if ye do not forgive, neither will your

Father which is in heaven forgive your trespasses.

ROMANS 4:17,19-21
17 (As it is written, I have made thee a father of many nations,) before him whom he believed, even God, who quickeneth the dead, and calleth those things which be not as though they were....
19 And being not weak in faith, he considered not his own body now dead, when he was about an hundred years old, neither yet the deadness of Sarah's womb:
20 He staggered not at the promise of God through unbelief; but was strong in faith, giving glory to God;
21 And being fully persuaded that, what he had promised, he was able also to perform.

ROMANS 10:17
17 So then faith cometh by hearing, and hearing by the word of God.

1 TIMOTHY 6:12
12 Fight the good fight of faith, lay hold on eternal life, whereunto thou art also called, and hast professed a good profession before many witnesses.

HEBREWS 11:1
1　Now faith is the substance of things hoped for, the evidence of things not seen....

HEBREWS 11:6

6   But without faith it is impossible to please him: for he that cometh to God must believe that he is, and that he is a rewarder of them that diligently seek him.

1 JOHN 5:4,5

4   For whatsoever is born of God overcometh the world: and this is the victory that overcometh the world, even our faith.

5   Who is he that overcometh the world, but he that believeth that Jesus is the Son of God?

God Wants Our Bodies Well!

1 CORINTHIANS 3:16

16 Know ye not that ye are the temple of God, and that the Spirit of God dwelleth in you?

ROMANS 8:2

2   For the law of the Spirit of life in Christ Jesus hath made me free from the law of sin and death.

1 JOHN 4:4

4   Ye are of God, little children, and have overcome them: because greater is he that is in you, than he that is in the world.

ROMANS 8:11

11 But if the Spirit of him that raised up Jesus from the dead dwell in you, he that raised up

Christ from the dead shall also quicken your mortal bodies by his Spirit that dwelleth in you.

PHILIPPIANS 2:13
13 For it is God which worketh in you both to will and to do of his good pleasure.

JAMES 4:7
7 Submit yourselves therefore to God. Resist the devil, and he will flee from you.

2 TIMOTHY 1:7
7 For God hath not given us the spirit of fear; but of power, and of love, and of a sound mind.

HEBREWS 2:14,15
14 Forasmuch then as the children are partakers of flesh and blood, he also himself likewise took part of the same; that through death he might destroy him that had the power of death, that is, the devil;
15 And deliver them who through fear of death [that is, the devil] **were all their lifetime subject to bondage.**

ROMANS 6:14
14 **For sin** [or Satan] **shall not have dominion over you: for ye are not under the law, but under grace.**

God's Word Is Unchanging

MATTHEW 4:4
4   But he answered and said, It is written, Man shall not live by bread alone, but by every word that proceedeth out of the mouth of God.

MATTHEW 8:16
16 When the even was come, they brought unto him many that were possessed with devils: and he cast out the spirits with his word, and healed all that were sick.

JOHN 1:1,14
1   In the beginning was the Word, and the Word was with God, and the Word was God. . . .
14 And the Word was made flesh, and dwelt among us, (and we beheld his glory, the glory as of the only begotten of the Father,) full of grace and truth.

JOHN 15:7
7   If ye abide in me, and my words abide in you, ye shall ask what ye will, and it shall be done unto you.

PSALM 107:20
20 He sent his word, and healed them, and delivered them from their destructions.

ISAIAH 55:11
11 So shall my word be that goeth forth out of my
mouth: it shall not return unto me void, but it
shall accomplish that which I please, and it shall
prosper in the thing whereto I sent it.

Confession Activates Your Faith

HEBREWS 4:14-16
14 Seeing then that we have a great high priest,
that is passed into the heavens, Jesus the Son of
God, let us hold fast our profession [or the margin
reads, Let us hold fast our *confession*].
15 For we have not an high priest which cannot
be touched with the feeling of our infirmities; but
was in all points tempted like as we are, yet with-
out sin.
16 Let us therefore come boldly unto the throne
of grace, that we may obtain mercy, and find
grace to help in time of need.

HEBREWS 10:23
23 Let us hold fast the profession [the margin
reads, Let us hold fast the *confession*] **of our faith**
without wavering; (for he is faithful that
promised;)

HEBREWS 10:35,36
35 Cast not away therefore your confidence,
which hath great recompence of reward.
36 For ye have need of patience, that, after ye

have done the will of God, ye might receive the promise.

PHILEMON 1:6
6   That the communication of thy mouth faith may become effectual by the acknowledging of every good thing which is in you in Christ Jesus.

REVELATION 12:11
11 And they overcame him by the blood of the Lamb, and by the word of their testimony. . . .

JOEL 3:10
10 . . . let the weak say, I am strong.

Chapter 4
The Blessings of the Law

Now read the entire chapters of Deuteronomy 28 and Galatians 3. Deuteronomy 28:1-14 contains the blessing for keeping the commandments of God's Law.

DEUTERONOMY 28:1-14

1 And it shall come to pass, if thou shalt hearken diligently unto the voice of the Lord thy God, to observe and to do all his commandments which I command thee this day, that the Lord thy God will set thee on high above all nations of the earth:

2 And all these blessings shall come on thee, and overtake thee, if thou shalt hearken unto the voice of the Lord thy God.

3 Blessed shalt thou be in the city, and blessed shalt thou be in the field.

4 Blessed shall be the fruit of thy body, and the fruit of thy ground, and the fruit of thy cattle, the increase of thy kine, and the flocks of thy sheep.

5 Blessed shall be thy basket and thy store.

6 Blessed shalt thou be when thou comest in, and blessed shalt thou be when thou goest out.

7 The Lord shall cause thine enemies that rise up against thee to be smitten before thy face: they shall come out against thee one way, and flee before thee seven ways.

8   The Lord shall command the blessing upon
thee in thy storehouses, and in all that thou
settest thine hand unto; and he shall bless thee in
the land which the Lord thy God giveth thee.
9   The Lord shall establish thee an holy people
unto himself, as he hath sworn unto thee, if thou
shalt keep the commandments of the Lord thy
God, and walk in his ways.
10 And all people of the earth shall see that thou
art called by the name of the Lord; and they shall
be afraid of thee.
11 And the Lord shall make thee plenteous in
goods, in the fruit of thy body, and in the fruit of
thy cattle, and in the fruit of thy ground, in the
land which the Lord sware unto thy fathers to
give thee.
12 The Lord shall open unto thee his good trea-
sure, the heaven to give the rain unto thy land in
his season, and to bless all the work of thine
hand: and thou shalt lend unto many nations, and
thou shalt not borrow.
13 And the Lord shall make thee the head, and
not the tail; and thou shalt be above only, and
thou shalt not be beneath; if that thou hearken
unto the commandments of the Lord thy God,
which I command thee this day, to observe and to
do them:
14 And thou shalt not go aside from any of the
words which I command thee this day, to the
right hand, or to the left, to go after other gods to
serve them.

The Curses of the Law

What is the curse of the Law? The only way to find out is to go back to the Law. The expression "the Law" as found in the New Testament usually refers to the Pentateuch, the first five books of the Bible.

As we go back to these books — to the Law — we find that the curse or punishment for breaking God's Law is threefold: poverty, sickness, and spiritual death. You can readily see that in the following scriptures. Deuteronomy 28:15-56 contains the curses for breaking the commandments of God's Law.

DEUTERONOMY 28:15-68
15 But it shall come to pass, if thou wilt not hearken unto the voice of the Lord thy God, to observe to do all his commandments and his statutes which I command thee this day; that all these curses shall come upon thee, and overtake thee:
16 Cursed shalt thou be in the city, and cursed shalt thou be in the field.
17 Cursed shall be thy basket and thy store.
18 Cursed shall be the fruit of thy body, and the fruit of thy land, the increase of thy kine, and the flocks of thy sheep.
19 Cursed shalt thou be when thou comest in, and cursed shalt thou be when thou goest out.
20 The Lord shall send upon thee cursing, vexation, and rebuke, in all that thou settest thine hand unto for to do, until thou be destroyed, and until thou perish quickly; because of the wicked-

ness of thy doings, whereby thou hast forsaken me.
21 The Lord shall make the pestilence cleave
unto thee, until he have consumed thee from off
the land, whither thou goest to possess it.
22 The Lord shall smite thee with a consumption,
and with a fever, and with an inflammation, and
with an extreme burning, and with the sword,
and with blasting, and with mildew; and they
shall pursue thee until thou perish.
23 And thy heaven that is over thy head shall be
brass, and the earth that is under thee shall be
iron.
24 The Lord shall make the rain of thy land pow-
der and dust: from heaven shall it come down
upon thee, until thou be destroyed.
25 The Lord shall cause thee to be smitten before
thine enemies: thou shalt go out one way against
them, and flee seven ways before them: and shalt
be removed into all the kingdoms of the earth.
26 And thy carcase shall be meat unto all fowls of
the air, and unto the beasts of the earth, and no
man shall fray them away.
27 The Lord will smite thee with the botch of
Egypt, and with the emerods, and with the scab,
and with the itch, whereof thou canst not be
healed.
28 The Lord shall smite thee with madness, and
blindness, and astonishment of heart:
29 And thou shalt grope at noonday, as the blind
gropeth in darkness, and thou shalt not prosper
in thy ways: and thou shalt be only oppressed and

spoiled evermore, and no man shall save thee.

30 Thou shalt betroth a wife, and another man shall lie with her: thou shalt build an house, and thou shalt not dwell therein: thou shalt plant a vineyard, and shalt not gather the grapes thereof.

31 Thine ox shall be slain before thine eyes, and thou shalt not eat thereof: thine ass shall be violently taken away from before thy face, and shall not be restored to thee: thy sheep shall be given unto thine enemies, and thou shalt have none to rescue them.

32 Thy sons and thy daughters shall be given unto another people, and thine eyes shall look, and fail with longing for them all the day long: and there shall be no might in thine hand.

33 The fruit of thy land, and all thy labours, shall a nation which thou knowest not eat up; and thou shalt be only oppressed and crushed alway:

34 So that thou shalt be mad for the sight of thine eyes which thou shalt see.

35 The Lord shall smite thee in the knees, and in the legs, with a sore botch that cannot be healed, from the sole of thy foot unto the top of thy head.

36 The Lord shall bring thee, and thy king which thou shalt set over thee, unto a nation which neither thou nor thy fathers have known; and there shalt thou serve other gods, wood and stone.

37 And thou shalt become an astonishment, a proverb, and a byword, among all nations whither the Lord shall lead thee.

38 Thou shalt carry much seed out into the field,

and shalt gather but little in; for the locust shall consume it.

39 Thou shalt plant vineyards, and dress them, but shalt neither drink of the wine, nor gather the grapes; for the worms shall eat them.

40 Thou shalt have olive trees throughout all thy coasts, but thou shalt not anoint thyself with the oil; for thine olive shall cast his fruit.

41 Thou shalt beget sons and daughters, but thou shalt not enjoy them; for they shall go into captivity.

42 All thy trees and fruit of thy land shall the locust consume.

43 The stranger that is within thee shall get up above thee very high; and thou shalt come down very low.

44 He shall lend to thee, and thou shalt not lend to him: he shall be the head, and thou shalt be the tail.

45 Moreover all these curses shall come upon thee, and shall pursue thee, and overtake thee, till thou be destroyed; because thou hearkenedst not unto the voice of the Lord thy God, to keep his commandments and his statutes which he commanded thee:

46 And they shall be upon thee for a sign and for a wonder, and upon thy seed for ever.

47 Because thou servedst not the Lord thy God with joyfulness, and with gladness of heart, for the abundance of all things;

48 Therefore shalt thou serve thine enemies which the Lord shall send against thee, in hunger,

and in thirst, and in nakedness, and in want of all things: and he shall put a yoke of iron upon thy neck, until he have destroyed thee.

49 The Lord shall bring a nation against thee from far, from the end of the earth, as swift as the eagle flieth; a nation whose tongue thou shalt not understand;

50 A nation of fierce countenance, which shall not regard the person of the old, nor shew favour to the young:

51 And he shall eat the fruit of thy cattle, and the fruit of thy land, until thou be destroyed: which also shall not leave thee either corn, wine, or oil, or the increase of thy kine, or flocks of thy sheep, until he have destroyed thee.

52 And he shall besiege thee in all thy gates, until thy high and fenced walls come down, wherein thou trustedst, throughout all thy land: and he shall besiege thee in all thy gates throughout all thy land, which the Lord thy God hath given thee.

53 And thou shalt eat the fruit of thine own body, the flesh of thy sons and of thy daughters, which the Lord thy God hath given thee, in the siege, and in the straitness, wherewith thine enemies shall distress thee:

54 So that the man that is tender among you, and very delicate, his eye shall be evil toward his brother, and toward the wife of his bosom, and toward the remnant of his children which he shall leave:

55 So that he will not give to any of them of the

flesh of his children whom he shall eat: because
he hath nothing left him in the siege, and in the
straitness, wherewith thine enemies shall distress thee in all thy gates.

56 The tender and delicate woman among you,
which would not adventure to set the sole of her
foot upon the ground for delicateness and tender-
ness, her eye shall be evil toward the husband of
her bosom, and toward her son, and toward her
daughter,

57 And toward her young one that cometh out
from between her feet, and toward her children
which she shall bear: for she shall eat them for
want of all things secretly in the siege and straitness, wherewith thine enemy shall distress thee
in thy gates.

58 If thou wilt not observe to do all the words of
this law that are written in this book, that thou
mayest fear this glorious and fearful name, the
Lord thy God;

59 Then the Lord will make thy plagues wonder-
ful, and the plagues of thy seed, even great
plagues, and of long continuance, and sore sicknesses, and of long continuance.

60 Moreover he will bring upon thee all the diseases of Egypt, which thou wast afraid of; and
they shall cleave unto thee.

61 Also every sickness, and every plague, which is
not written in the book of this law, them will the
Lord bring upon thee, until thou be destroyed.

62 And ye shall be left few in number, whereas ye

were as the stars of heaven for multitude; because thou wouldest not obey the voice of the Lord thy God.

63 And it shall come to pass, that as the Lord rejoiced over you to do you good, and to multiply you; so the Lord will rejoice over you to destroy you, and to bring you to nought; and ye shall be plucked from off the land whither thou goest to possess it.

64 And the Lord shall scatter thee among all people, from the one end of the earth even unto the other; and there thou shalt serve other gods, which neither thou nor thy fathers have known, even wood and stone.

65 And among these nations shalt thou find no ease, neither shall the sole of thy foot have rest: but the Lord shall give thee there a trembling heart, and failing of eyes, and sorrow of mind:

66 And thy life shall hang in doubt before thee; and thou shalt fear day and night, and shalt have none assurance of thy life:

67 In the morning thou shalt say, Would God it were even! and at even thou shalt say, Would God it were morning! for the fear of thine heart wherewith thou shalt fear, and for the sight of thine eyes which thou shalt see.

68 And the Lord shall bring thee into Egypt again with ships, by the way whereof I spake unto thee, Thou shalt see it no more again: and there ye shall be sold unto your enemies for bondmen and bondwomen, and no man shall buy you.

We Are Redeemed From the Curse of the Law

Now let's look at Galatians chapter 3 and see who we are in Christ and what we have in Him. Christ has redeemed us from the curse of the Law.

GALATIANS 3:1-29
1   O foolish Galatians, who hath bewitched you, that ye should not obey the truth, before whose eyes Jesus Christ hath been evidently set forth, crucified among you?
2   This only would I learn of you, Received ye the Spirit by the works of the law, or by the hearing of faith?
3   Are ye so foolish? having begun in the Spirit, are ye now made perfect by the flesh?
4   Have ye suffered so many things in vain? if it be yet in vain.
5   He therefore that ministereth to you the Spirit, and worketh miracles among you, doeth he it by the works of the law, or by the hearing of faith?
6   Even as Abraham believed God, and it was accounted to him for righteousness.
7   Know ye therefore that they which are of faith, the same are the children of Abraham.
8   And the scripture, foreseeing that God would justify the heathen through faith, preached before the gospel unto Abraham, saying, In thee shall all nations be blessed.
9   So then they which be of faith are blessed with faithful Abraham.

10 For as many as are of the works of the law are under the curse: for it is written, Cursed is every one that continueth not in all things which are written in the book of the law to do them.

11 But that no man is justified by the law in the sight of God, it is evident: for, The just shall live by faith.

12 And the law is not of faith: but, The man that doeth them shall live in them.

13 Christ hath redeemed us from the curse of the law, being made a curse for us: for it is written, Cursed is every one that hangeth on a tree:

14 That the blessing of Abraham might come on the Gentiles through Jesus Christ; that we might receive the promise of the Spirit through faith.

15 Brethren, I speak after the manner of men; Though it be but a man's covenant, yet if it be confirmed, no man disannulleth, or addeth thereto.

16 Now to Abraham and his seed were the promises made. He saith not, And to seeds, as of many; but as of one, And to thy seed, which is Christ.

17 And this I say, that the covenant, that was confirmed before of God in Christ, the law, which was four hundred and thirty years after, cannot disannul, that it should make the promise of none effect.

18 For if the inheritance be of the law, it is no more of promise: but God gave it to Abraham by promise.

19 Wherefore then serveth the law? It was added because of transgressions, till the seed should come to whom the promise was made; and it was ordained by angels in the hand of a mediator.

20 Now a mediator is not a mediator of one, but God is one.

21 Is the law then against the promises of God? God forbid: for if there had been a law given which could have given life, verily righteousness should have been by the law.

22 But the scripture hath concluded all under sin, that the promise by faith of Jesus Christ might be given to them that believe.

23 But before faith came, we were kept under the law, shut up unto the faith which should afterwards be revealed.

24 Wherefore the law was our schoolmaster to bring us unto Christ, that we might be justified by faith.

25 But after that faith is come, we are no longer under a schoolmaster.

26 For ye are all the children of God by faith in Christ Jesus.

27 For as many of you as have been baptized into Christ have put on Christ.

28 There is neither Jew nor Greek, there is neither bond nor free, there is neither male nor female: for ye are all one in Christ Jesus.

29 And if ye be Christ's, then are ye Abraham's seed, and heirs according to the promise.

Christ has redeemed us from the curse of the Law. We know sickness is a part of the curse of the Law. But notice that according to these scriptures, specifically Deuteronomy 28:61, that *every* sickness is a curse of the Law.

DEUTERONOMY 28:61
61 Also EVERY SICKNESS, and EVERY PLAGUE, which is not written in the book of this law, them will the Lord bring upon thee, until thou be destroyed.

Notice it said, "*. . . every sickness, and every plague, which is NOT WRITTEN in the book of this law. . . .*" There are a number of diseases that are listed in Deuteronomy 28, but then in verse 61 it also adds, "*. . . EVERY SICKNESS, and EVERY PLAGUE. . . .*"

Therefore, whatever your sickness is — cancer tuberculosis, anemia, mental distress, and so forth — you can say, "According to Deuteronomy 28:61, my sickness is a curse of the Law."

Now notice Galatians 3:13 again.

GALATIANS 3:13
13 CHRIST HATH REDEEMED US FROM THE CURSE OF THE LAW being made a curse for us, For it is written, Cursed is everyone that hangeth on a tree that the blessing of Abraham might come on the Gentiles through Jesus Christ, that we might receive the promise of the Spirit through faith.

Take Your Medicine!

This is what I want you to confess: (Say it over and over again to yourself. Say it out loud if you're by yourself; say it quietly to yourself if someone else is with you.)

Confession

"According to Deuteronomy 28:61, my sickness, (name your sickness, whether it's cancer, tuberculosis, kidney trouble, liver trouble — whatever it is), is a curse of the Law. But according to Galatians 3:13, Christ has *redeemed* me from the curse of the Law. Therefore, I confess I am redeemed from _____" (specify the sickness).

I'll give you an illustration. Let's say your sickness is cancer. *You* say: "According to Deuteronomy 28:61, my sickness, cancer, is a curse of the Law. But according to Galatians 3:13, Christ has redeemed me from the curse of the Law. Therefore, He's redeemed me from the curse of sickness. Therefore, I confess I am redeemed from cancer."

Or suppose your trouble is a stomach ulcer. Then say this: "According to Deuteronomy 28:61, my sickness, stomach ulcer, is a curse of the Law. But according to Galatians 3:13, Christ has redeemed me from the curse of the Law. Therefore, I confess I am redeemed from ulcers of the stomach."

Or, for instance, suppose your condition is a blood

disease. You say: "According to Deuteronomy 28:61, my blood disease is a curse of the Law. But according to Galatians 3:13, Christ has redeemed me from the curse of the Law. Therefore, I confess I am redeemed from blood disease."

I just gave you those examples as an illustration. Whatever your sickness is, call it a curse of the Law. Confess that it's a curse of the Law. Then confess Galatians 3:13: "Christ has redeemed me from the curse of the Law. Therefore, I am redeemed from _____" (and specify the sickness).

Chapter 5
God's Medicine Works!
A Real-Life Illustration

Dr. Lilian B. Yeomans, a medical doctor and surgeon, received divine healing after becoming ill to the point of death due to a narcotic addiction. Medical science couldn't do anything to help her. She came right down to death's door, and medical science told her she had to die.

But then someone told her the account recorded in the Bible about Jesus healing the woman with the issue of blood (Mark 5:25-34). Dr. Yeomans had been in a backslidden condition for several years at this time. But when she heard about the woman with the issue of blood who was healed, Dr. Yeomans got back into fellowship with God. Then she received healing and was raised up from her deathbed.

After being raised up from a deathbed and realizing that divine healing is right and good, Dr. Yeomans began to preach and teach divine healing from the Word, and she did that for many years. In one of her books, she talked about enjoying forty-three years of divine health.

In the course of time, Dr. Yeomans and her sister bought a large home with money they had inherited from their parents' estate. They turned the house into what they called a "faith home"; that is, they would take people in who were sick so they could get them healed by God's divine power through faith in His Word.

All the people they ministered to were terminally ill or incurable. In other words, doctors had given nearly every one of them up to die; they were all beyond the aid of medical science. Yet Dr. Yeomans and her sister rarely lost a case. They got most of them healed.

Dr. Yeomans got these people healed by doing what I'm telling you to do. She would read scriptures on divine healing to them and tell them to confess them over and over again to themselves.

Dr. Yeomans and her sister could only take three or four sick people at a time into their faith home, so they had a waiting list. In one case in particular, a woman who had been on the list came to them who had tuberculosis. When the woman arrived at the faith home by ambulance, Dr. Yeomans checked her pulse and knew the woman was in a dying condition.

In fact, Dr. Yeomans said if she'd still been practicing medicine, she would have immediately begun to administer a strong stimulant to stimulate the woman's heart action. But Dr. Yeomans didn't have a license to practice medicine in the particular state they were in, so she just had the dying woman taken to one of the bedrooms.

Dr. Yeomans related: "I sat by the bedside and read to her from my Bible. I said to her, 'Close your eyes and rest and just listen to the Word.'" And for two hours Dr. Yeomans read healing scriptures, like the ones contained in this book. Instead of giving this woman a shot to stimulate her heart, she gave her a dose of *God's* medicine — His Word!

Dr. Yeomans had all the scriptures on the subject of

healing marked in her Bible, and she read healing scriptures to this woman from Genesis to Revelation. Notice she didn't read scriptures to her on the subject of water baptism. That dying woman didn't need to hear about water baptism! That wouldn't heal her. No, she needed to hear about *healing*.

This woman didn't need to hear about the message of the remission of sin and the new birth. The woman was already saved. She had accepted her salvation.

The woman needed to hear about what *she needed* — divine healing. And, thank God, God's Word provides for every need.

Dr. Yeomans related: "I had read to her the entire chapter of Deuteronomy 28 and Galatians 3. Then I read other healing scriptures, but I reread these two chapters to her over and over again.

"Then I asked her, 'Did you notice that according to Deuteronomy 28:22, that consumption, or tuberculosis, is a curse of the Law? But did you also notice that according to Galatians 3:13, Christ has redeemed us from the curse of the Law? Therefore, He has redeemed you from tuberculosis.'"

In those days tuberculosis was one of the biggest causes of death in America. That was before the days of miracle drugs and advanced medical technology. This woman was in the last stages of the disease and was virtually dead as she lay there on the bed in that faith home.

Dr. Yeomans instructed the woman, "At every waking moment, repeat out loud, 'According to Deuteron-

omy 28:22, consumption or tuberculosis is a curse of the
Law. But according to Galatians 3:13, Christ has
redeemed me from the curse of the Law. So Christ has
redeemed me from tuberculosis.'"

The next morning Dr. Yeomans and her sister read
healing scriptures to each of the four patients who were
in their faith home. Dr. Yeomans said to the woman
with tuberculosis, "Did you say what I told you to say
last night?"

"Yes," the woman answered. "It seems like I didn't
even sleep ten minutes; I must have said it ten thousand times. But it still doesn't mean a thing in the
world to me."

"That's all right," Dr. Yeomans said, "just keep saying it. Say, 'According to Deuteronomy 28:22, consumption or tuberculosis is a curse of the Law. But according
to Galatians 3:13 Christ has redeemed me from the
curse of the Law. So Christ has redeemed me from
tuberculosis.'"

The woman with tuberculosis continued to take
God's medicine. When Dr. Yeomans went to her room to
read to her the next morning, she asked the woman,
"Are you saying what I told you to say?"

"Yes," the woman answered. "It seemed like I didn't
sleep but ten minutes last night. I must have quoted
those scriptures ten thousand times. But they still don't
mean a thing to me. I don't feel like I'm getting anything out of it."

"That's all right," Dr. Yeomans replied, "just keep
saying it. Keep repeating it to yourself." The woman

was so weak and so far gone physically, she couldn't say it very loudly, so she just said it quietly to herself.

Afterward, Dr. Yeomans and her sister were in the kitchen cooking the noon meal when they heard some commotion upstairs in one of the bedrooms. It sounded like somebody had hit the floor and was running. All the patients had been bedfast and virtually dead, but one of them was up and out of bed and running. And she was calling, "Dr. Yeomans! Dr. Yeomans!"

Dr. Yeomans rushed out of the kitchen, and this woman who'd been dying of tuberculosis was rushing down the steps, hollering, "Dr. Yeomans! Did you know I'm healed? I'm healed! I'm the one who had the tuberculosis, but I'm healed!"

"Yes, I know it!" Dr. Yeomans replied. "I've been trying to tell you that for almost three days now."

What happened to this woman who was dying just days before? The Word she had been confessing got down into her spirit. It wasn't some magic potion that Dr. Yeomans gave her. And it wasn't Dr. Yeomans' great personality or abilities bestowed on her by God that got that woman healed. No, it was just the *Word*! It was just faith in God's Word that healed the woman and raised her off her deathbed.

You see, Dr. Yeomans knew that eventually the truth of God's Word would register on the woman's heart. Many times, folks are just sitting around waiting for somebody else to do something for them. They're waiting for a healing evangelist to get them healed or for the Spirit of God to manifest Himself and heal them by a gift of the Spirit (1 Cor. 12:1-11).

But the Holy Spirit may or may not manifest Himself in that way. We don't control spiritual gifts; only God does. The manifestation of the Holy Spirit is divided to every man severally as He wills (1 Cor. 12:11). The Holy Spirit manifests Himself occasionally to one here and one there. And God does that as a sign to get a person's attention so he'll know God's alive and working and so the person will start believing Him.

However, if you just sit around and wait for a manifestation of the Holy Spirit to come to you, it may never come. But I'll tell you one thing about it — God's Word *always* works.

God's Word works! I challenge you to take these same scriptures in this book, especially Deuteronomy 28 and Galatians 3, and feed on them. Get them into your spirit by constantly meditating on them and saying them over and over to yourself. God's Word is medicine, so *take your medicine*! His Word will become life to you and healing to all your flesh.